Red Ribbon Rosie

By Jean Marzollo

Illustrated by Blanche Sims

A STEPPING STONE BOOK

Random House New York

To the girls and boys in Ms. Radtke's third-grade class who helped me: Abby Barton, Jill Bono, Christine Jamin, Elena LaDue, Kelly Pilner, Silvia Scanga, Katie Sedlacek, Danielle Tuttle, Monica Weise, Jay Baxter, John Betros, Joey Chiarella, Gino Forgione, Seth Knapp, B. J. LeMon, Matthew Perpetua, Michael Powell, Joshua Procida, Keith Sexton, Scott Tangen, and, last but not least, Bret Varricchio.

—J. M.

Text copyright © 1988 by Jean Marzollo. Illustrations copyright © 1988 by Blanche Sims. All rights reserved under International and Pan-American Copyright Conventions. Published in the United States by Random House, Inc., New York, and simultaneously in Canada by Random House of Canada Limited, Toronto.

Library of Congress Cataloging-in-Publication Data:
Marzollo, Jean. Red Ribbon Rosie / by Jean Marzollo ; illustrated by Blanche Sims. p. cm.—(A Stepping stone book) SUMMARY: Rosie's decision to cheat in order to win a race with her best friend, Sally, has disastrous results until her older sister helps her learn an important lesson about winning races and keeping friends. ISBN: 0-394-89608-4 (pbk.); 0-394-99608-9 (lib. bdg.) [1. Friendship—Fiction. 2. Conduct of life—Fiction.] I. Sims, Blanche, ill. II. Title. PZ7.M3688Rd 1988 [Fic]—dc19 87-29641

Manufactured in the United States of America 3 4 5 6 7 8 9 0

Contents

1.

Gym Class Jitters

"Ready," said Mr. Mac, the gym teacher.

Rosie stood alert at the starting line next to her best friend, Sally. It was a cool, sunny day in June, a perfect day for the 100-yard dash.

"On your mark," said Mr. Mac.

Rosie, Sally, and the other kids in the heat crouched down.

"Get set," said Mr. Mac.

Rosie, Sally, and the other kids got up on their toes, ready to spring.

"Go!"

Rosie and Sally took off like bullets. As usual, they were ahead of everyone else. Seconds later, the two girls crossed the finish line. As usual, Sally was first and Rosie was second.

"Right on, Sally!" someone shouted. Rosie turned. Sam and Chris were cheering for Sally on the sidelines. Sally bowed to them like a famous ballerina. Rosie felt like bowing like a ballerina, too, but she didn't know if she should because she had only come in second.

Just once, she thought to herself, *I'd like to win.*

But the idea of trying to beat Sally gave Rosie the jitters. The jitters were a jumpy, nervous feeling. Sometimes Rosie got the jitters from watching scary shows on TV. Sometimes she got them after a nightmare. She had them now because she was afraid of being mad at her best friend. Why did Sally always have to beat her? It wasn't fair. Rosie was a good runner, and she loved to race. But no matter how fast she ran, Sally ran faster. Rosie didn't like the way that made her feel.

To get rid of the jitters, Rosie rubbed her arms and shook her shoulders. Then she did a cartwheel. It was a pretty good cartwheel, with her legs almost straight.

"Watch me," said Sally. Rosie watched her friend turn a perfect cartwheel.

"How was that?" asked Sally.

"So-so," said Rosie.

Sally looked at her in surprise.

"Only kidding," said Rosie, laughing. "It was perfect, as usual."

Mr. Mac blew his whistle and said, "Okay, kids, gather 'round." He sat down on the grass. Rosie and Sally took each other's hand and went over to him. They sat on the grass with the other kids in a big circle around Mr. Mac.

Mr. Mac looked like a skinny Santa Claus in sweat pants. His hair was so blond it was almost white, and he had a big mustache and a bushy beard. Sometimes the third graders called him Mr. MacClaus, but Mr. Mac didn't like that name. "Don't call me Mr. MacClaus," he said. "Or you'll ruin the surprise." Every year Mr. Mac stuffed a big pillow under his shirt and dressed up as Santa Claus for the kindergarten Christmas party. The little kids never recognized him, he said.

Right now Mr. Mac was holding his clipboard against his chest and waiting. He was staring at Sam and Chris, who were poking each other and giggling. The rest of the third graders began to stare at Sam and Chris too. Sam and Chris lived on Rosie's street and were her friends, so she said, "Chris! Sam! Cool it!"

When they saw everyone looking at them,

Chris and Sam sat up and became perfectly quiet. Mr. Mac winked at Rosie and said, "Thank you. Now, I have an important announcement to make."

"Is it about Field Day?" asked Chris. Since it was June, he and everyone else had been wondering when Field Day would be.

"Yes," said Mr. Mac. "Field Day will take place this Friday."

"Hooray!" everyone shouted.

Mr. Mac described what the third graders would do. "You'll compete against each other, and members of the other grades will compete against members of *their* grades. Today's Monday. Tomorrow you'll start practicing the third-grade Field Day events. By Friday you should be ready."

Rosie felt a rush of excitement. She loved Field Day! But then she had a disturbing thought. On Field Day, Sally would beat her in every race. Rosie didn't want that to happen. She wanted to beat Sally, at least once. Could she do it? And was it nice to want to beat your best friend? Rosie felt nervous and jumpy again. Her jitters were back, this time worse than ever.

2.

Two Teams Is Too Many

Mr. Mac stood up. "Count off in twos," he said. "Rosie, would you please start?"

"One," said Rosie.

"Two," said Sally.

"One," said Chris.

"Two," said Sam.

"One," said Marco.

"Two," said Billy.

As Rosie listened to the rest of the kids, she wondered why Mr. Mac was having them count off. Gym class was almost over. Suddenly she understood. They were counting off to make their Field Day teams. Since Rosie was a One and Sally was a Two, they would be on separate teams! That was terrible!

Or was it? If she and Sally were on separate teams, then she would be racing against Sally.

It would be okay to want to beat her, even if Sally was her best friend.

When the count-off was over, Mr. Mac said, "Would the Ones please stand on my left? And the Twos please stand on my right?"

Rosie went with Chris and Marco and the other Ones to stand on Mr. Mac's left. Sally went with Sam and Billy and the rest of the Twos to stand on his right.

"These are the two third-grade teams for Field Day," said Mr. Mac. "On Friday each team can earn points by winning the field events. The field events will be: the sack race, the three-legged race, the mystery toss, and the long race. Each team can also earn points for sportsman-ship, for the best team name, and for the best team costumes. The team that earns the most points at the end of the day will win. Everyone on that team will get a blue ribbon. Everyone on the other team will get a red ribbon."

"Let's be the Blue Ribbon Bears!" said Chris, starting to growl like a bear.

"Or the Blue Ribbon Broncos!" said Marco, neighing like a horse.

"You'll have plenty of time to discuss your team names," said Mr. Mac. "One last thing: Make your costumes so that you can put them on over your gym clothes at lunchtime for the costume contest. You'll have to take them off afterward so that you can run in the afternoon event. It might make sense to have your jer-seys and shorts be part of your costume. Any questions?"

"Can our parents come and watch?" asked Billy.

"Yes," said Mr. Mac. "I'll be sending a note home."

"Can we wear makeup?" asked Sally.

"If it doesn't interfere with racing and eating," said Mr. Mac.

"Can we roast marshmallows?" asked Chris.

"Parents will be serving lunch," said Mr. Mac. "I don't think marshmallows are on the menu."

"Can we switch places on teams so we can be with our friends?" asked Sally. "I want to be with Rosie."

"No," said Mr. Mac. "You're all friends no matter what team you're on, and no matter who wins or loses."

There were more questions, but everyone was too excited to sit calmly. So Mr. Mac let the third graders go back to the school building. The Ones walked with the Ones, and the Twos walked with the Twos.

Chris couldn't stop talking. "I've got so many ideas for names!" he told Rosie. "We could be the Pirates or the Jets or the Mariners!"

"Texas Rangers!" said Marco. "They play near Mexico!" Marco was from Mexico. He had come to live with his cousin Sam for the year.

"Those are names of pro-ball teams," said

Rosie. "Do we want to win Field Day or not?"

"Of course we want to win," said Marco.

"Then we're going to need every point we can get, including the point for the best team name."

"How about the Raiders or the Giants?" asked Chris. He didn't understand what Rosie was getting at.

"Chris," said Rosie. "I know you know a lot of good team names, but those real names won't help us win. We need to think of a team name that's never been used before. Something original."

"Okay," said Chris. "Let's go home and sleep on it."

When they were near the school, Sally ran over to Rosie. "I wish we were on the same team!" she said, looking sad.

"I know what you mean," said Rosie. "But remember what Mr. MacClaus said. We're all friends, no matter what." Rosie put her arm around her best friend and hoped that Mr. MacClaus was right.

3.

Around the Block with Ben

After school, Rosie and Sally walked home together. "The Twos will probably win," said Sally. "We've got the best athletes—Sam and Billy and, well, you know. . . ."

"I know—you've got you," said Rosie. She had been thinking the same thing—the Twos were a better team than the Ones. "But you never can tell," said Rosie. "The Ones are very original."

"Have you thought of a good name?" asked Sally. "The Twos can't think of one."

Rosie smiled mysteriously. She didn't want to admit that the Ones hadn't thought of a good name yet either.

"Call your grandma," said Sally when they reached her house. "See if you can stay for a while."

Rosie called her grandma as Sally pulled two yogurts and a carton of apple juice out of the refrigerator.

Rosie's grandma said she could stay. As Rosie hung up the phone, Sally's big brother, Ben, came into the kitchen. "Hiya, Poodle," he said to Sally, ruffling her hair. "Hiya, Toodle," he said to Rosie, tugging one of her braids. Those were his own personal nicknames for Sally and Rosie. No one else besides Ben called the girls Poodle and Toodle.

Rosie stared up at Ben, who was one of the

tallest people she had ever met. He was already home from college for the summer. At college Ben ran track and won lots of ribbons and trophies. Rosie and Sally sometimes went into his room to admire them. All Ben's ribbons were blue for first prize, except for one red ribbon for second prize. Rosie always wondered what had happened the day Ben came in second.

Just now, Ben was dressed in running clothes with a headband radio on his ears.

"You going running?" asked Rosie.

"Sure am," said Ben. "Want to come? I'm only going twelve miles today."

"That's too short a run for us," said Sally. "We're practicing for Field Day."

"Well, par-don *me,* Poodle!" said Ben, giving his sister a hug. Rosie felt a tug of jealousy. She wished she had an older brother, especially an older brother like Ben who won blue ribbons and wore a headband radio. All she had was a high-school-age sister named Jane who liked to make clothes on her sewing machine and hated sports.

"If you two want," said Ben, "I'll jog around the block with you once and give you a few pointers."

"Great!" said Rosie, putting her yogurt and apple juice back into the refrigerator. "When can we start?"

"You really want to go?" asked Sally.

"Yes!" said Rosie. "Don't you?"

"I go with him all the time," said Sally. "And every morning before school I jog with my mother. I think I'll stay home and finish my snack."

"Nobody in my family ever runs," said Rosie as she and Ben headed out the door.

While they ran around the block, Ben told Rosie that one of the most important things about running was paying attention. "You have to think as well as run," he said. "Think about your energy, especially in a long race. Energy is like money. You don't want to spend it all at once. Save some for the end of the race."

"What else do you have to think about?" asked Rosie.

"Think about the people you're racing against," said Ben. "Listen to where they are. But don't turn around to look for them, or you might fall down."

"What's the most important thing of all?" asked Rosie.

"Enjoy yourself," said Ben.

Rosie thought about that for a while. Then she asked, "What happened to you the day you won your red ribbon?"

"Which one?"

"The only red ribbon you ever won. It's on your bulletin board."

"Oh, that ribbon," said Ben. "I put that up because I liked that race. It was near the shore and I could smell the ocean as I ran. But I have a lot more red ribbons in a drawer, and white ones, too, for third prize. Did you think I always won?"

"Not really," said Rosie, even though she had.

"You're a good runner," said Ben. "You'll win some races too."

I'll have to beat your sister to do that, thought Rosie. But she didn't say a word.

4.

Practice Makes Perfect

On Tuesday morning Rosie, Chris, Marco, and the other Ones met at the playground to talk about their ideas for team names.

"The Devil Dogs," said Marco.

"That's a food," said Rosie.

"The Meatballs!" said Chris. "We can paint paper bag masks to look like meatballs."

"That's gross," said Marco. "And besides, meatballs are a food too. If we can't have Devil Dogs, we can't have Meatballs."

"I've got an idea," said Rosie. She looked around to make sure no Twos were listening. "The Firebirds," she whispered.

The kids looked at each other. "Not bad," said Chris. "But a Firebird's a car."

"I didn't think of that." Rosie was disappointed.

"But it's a neat name, and we could all wear red jerseys decorated with glitter," said a girl named Lily.

"We could make wings, too," a boy called T.J. said.

"And tails," said Rosie. "But if it's a car, it's not original."

"I got it!" said Chris. "The Fire Fish!"

"That's a good idea," said Marco, "but fish don't have wings."

"They have fins, though! We can be the Fabulous Flying Fire Fish!" said Chris. He was so excited his face turned fiery red.

"I like it," said Rosie.

So did everyone else.

Later on, in gym, Mr. Mac handed out sacks to everyone. "Today we'll practice the sack race," he said. "Put your legs in the sack and hold it up with your hands. See how long you can hop. The trick is: Don't run. Hop. This is just a practice session. Don't try to race."

Rosie pulled up her sack and started hopping. She was pretty good at it. At first she and Sally were hopping around next to each other, but then Sally started hopping toward

Sam. To catch up with her, Rosie started to run. Bam! She fell down. Sally was still hopping around like a jack rabbit. She hopped longer than everyone else.

The next day was Wednesday. "Today we're going to practice the three-legged race," said Mr. Mac. "Pick a partner who is on your team." Rosie and Marco picked each other to be partners. As Mr. Mac tied their ankles together he said, "Remember: Start off with your inside foot. And walk at first. If you stay together, you can speed up to a jog."

Everyone spread out in a line. "Ready . . . on your mark . . . get set . . . go!" yelled Mr. Mac.

Rosie and Marco started with their inside feet, and for one splendid moment they zipped across the field. Then Marco speeded up without telling Rosie, and they both fell down.

Rosie looked up from her worm's-eye view just as Sally and Billy whizzed by. They were racing Freddy and Chris, who were going fast too. Rosie glowered at Marco. "On Field Day please don't speed up without telling me!" she said as Sally and Billy won the race.

Mr. Mac asked the third graders to change partners for the mystery toss. This time Rosie and Chris decided to be partners. Rosie hoped Chris wouldn't be too silly.

Mr. Mac gave each couple a big rubber ball and said, "Toss the ball back and forth with your partner. Each time you catch it, step back one step."

Rosie threw the ball to Chris. He caught it and stepped back one step. Chris threw the ball to Rosie, who caught it and stepped back.

On and on they went until they were quite far apart. "We're doing great at this!" said Rosie.

"Practice makes perfect!" yelled Chris, but just as he said it he dropped the ball. Sally and Sam were still going at it, and they lasted longer than everyone else.

"It won't be so easy on Field Day," Mr. Mac told the kids, "because then you'll be catching something else."

"What is it?" asked Rosie.

But Mr. Mac wouldn't say. "It's a secret," he said. "If I told you, the mystery toss wouldn't be a mystery."

After school that day Sally walked home with Rosie. She was going to stay at Rosie's for the afternoon and for supper too. Rosie's grandma was making spaghetti sauce. The two girls sat in Rosie's kitchen, tasting little bowls of the delicious sauce and talking about Field Day.

"What's your team's name?" asked Rosie.

"I can't tell," said Sally. "But it's really cool. It's not silly or stupid or anything like that. Ben helped us think of it."

Rosie wondered if Sally and her brother Ben would think the Fabulous Flying Fire Fish was a stupid team name or if they would think it was cool.

"What's your name?" Sally asked.

"I'm not going to tell you *our* name if you're not going to tell me *your* name," said Rosie. "What do you think I am? A complete idiot?"

"Don't be so sensitive, Rosie," said her grandma.

"Well, what do you expect? Me to tell her our name when she won't tell me hers?"

"I expect you to be polite to your guests," said her grandma.

But Rosie didn't see why she had to be polite to Sally if Sally wasn't being polite to her.

"You want to play dress-up?" asked Sally.

"No," said Rosie.

"Want to play school?"

"No," said Rosie.

"Well, what do you want to do?" asked Sally.

"Nothing," said Rosie. She went into the living room and turned on the TV. Sally followed her and sat on the couch. Instead of sitting next to her, Rosie slumped down angrily in a chair. All she did was watch cartoons. She didn't even talk during commercials.

During the middle of a show, Rosie's older sister, Jane, came into the room. "How do you like this dress I'm making?" she asked, twirling around. The dress had a very short skirt with ruffles and big balloon sleeves.

"It's neat," said Sally.

"Jane, do you mind?" said Rosie. "We're in the middle of an important program."

"Grandma thinks it's too short," Jane told Sally.

"I think it's just right," said Sally. "You really made that all by yourself?"

"Sure. Want to come see my sewing machine?"

Sally and Jane left the room. Rosie watched a mouse beat up a cat on TV. A few minutes later Sally came back wearing a headband made of Jane's dress material.

"Do you like it?" she asked.

"It's okay," said Rosie, thinking to herself that Jane had never offered to make *her* a headband.

When Rosie's mother came home from work, she said, "You mean to tell me you two girls have been watching TV all afternoon? On such a beautiful day? Why didn't you go out and play? Why didn't you practice for Field Day?"

"I practice with my brother all the time," said Sally, helping Rosie's mother by taking a bag of groceries from her. "And every morning before school my mother jogs with me. Do you like to jog?"

"I can't stand it," said Rosie's mother. "But I like to play tennis and swim."

It's too bad, thought Rosie, *that tennis and swimming aren't sports that count on Field Day. How can I ever beat Sally when everyone in her family helps her and nobody in my family helps me?*

5.

Disaster

On Thursday Mr. Mac told the third graders, "Tomorrow's the big day, ladies and gentlemen! The third graders will have their events at the far end of the field. In the morning we'll have the sack race, the three-legged race, and the mystery toss. At lunchtime we'll have the names and costume contest. Is everybody ready?"

When they heard the word *costume,* some of the Twos started to giggle and whisper to each other. Rosie wondered if they had a funny costume. A funny costume would probably win.

Mr. Mac blew his whistle to calm the Twos down. "After lunch," he said, "the ten fastest third graders will race one lap around the big school track. Today we're going to find out who the ten fastest third-grade runners are. Everyone who wants to qualify should line up on the starting line now."

Rosie headed straight for the start. She knew she wouldn't win, but she was sure she would be one of the top ten. Sally came over and stood beside her. "Good luck," said Rosie. She was sorry that she had been so crabby the day before.

"Same to you," said Sally. Rosie was glad to see that Sally wasn't mad.

"Ready," said Mr. Mac.

Everyone on the line got ready.

"On your mark."

Everyone got down.

"Get set."

Everyone got up on their toes, ready to spring.

"Go!"

Much to her surprise, Rosie got a super start and pulled out way ahead of everyone, even Sally. Maybe she would come in first today! But halfway around the track she heard Sally call, "See you later, pal!" Sally flashed by Rosie and cut in front of her to the inside of the track. To win, Rosie would have to go around Sally the long way—on the outside. Rosie put on a burst of speed, but she couldn't do it. She just wasn't fast enough to pass Sally on the outside. And there was no room on the track to go around her on the inside.

Rosie listened. She didn't hear anyone coming up behind her. The other kids must be far behind. She and Sally were way ahead of everyone else. They were alone in the lead.

Suddenly Rosie had an idea that might help her win the race. Up ahead, on the grass inside the track, were some stacks of hurdles. She and Sally would be hidden from view—just for a moment—when they ran past the hurdles. In that moment Rosie could get around Sally by cutting across the grass.

It was cheating, but it could work. Mr. Mac wouldn't see. The other runners probably wouldn't either. And maybe Sally wouldn't notice. If she did notice, maybe she wouldn't mind. Maybe Sally would let Rosie beat her just this once. After all, this wasn't the *real* race. Rosie put one foot on the grass, then the other, and in seconds it was over.

"No fair!" yelled Sally. "You cut across the grass!"

But Rosie paid no attention to her. Far ahead

down the track she could see the finish line and her class. Rosie loved the feeling of knowing she was going to win. She felt so wonderful that she ran faster and faster. Rosie ran across the finish line with her hands in the air. Everyone cheered.

Then Sally came running up. "Rosie cut across the grass!" she yelled.

The cheering stopped. Rosie felt sick. Why did Sally have to tell on her?

"Is that true, Rosie?" asked Mr. Mac.

Rosie was so mad at Sally for telling that she couldn't speak. Then she realized that no one could prove Sally was telling the truth. No one could prove Rosie had cheated. It was Rosie's word against Sally's. All Rosie had to say was "Sally's lying," and she would be safe. But Rosie couldn't say anything—because Sally was telling the truth.

A moment ago, Rosie had been so happy. Now she was completely miserable.

"Rosie?" said Mr. Mac softly. "Did you cut across the grass?"

Rosie nodded yes. In a whisper she added, "I'm sorry."

"Sally came in first," said Mr. Mac in a loud

voice to everyone. "The next eight runners after her qualify." The kids who had made it cheered. Sally, Marco, Sam, and Billy were among them.

"But that only makes nine runners," said Sally. "Who's the tenth runner, Mr. Mac?"

Suddenly all the kids were quiet. They seemed to know how terrible Rosie felt.

Mr. Mac put his arm around Rosie and said to her, "Rosie, why did you cheat? You were going to be one of the top ten runners anyway."

"I wanted to know what it feels like to win," said Rosie. She was almost in tears.

"You wanted to win so much that you cheated," said Mr. Mac. "That was wrong, but I'm glad you told the truth. Because of that, you may be the tenth runner."

"All right!" shouted Chris.

"Hurray!" shouted Marco.

"I don't think it's fair," said Sally. "Rosie cheated."

"I know," said Mr. Mac. "But she learned a good lesson."

"Yeah, she learned she could win by cheating," said Sally.

"No," said Mr. Mac. "She learned that winning by cheating isn't fun at all."

After school, Sally walked home with Billy and Sam. Rosie ran to catch up with her. "Want to come over and play with me?" she asked.

"No," said Sally. "You're not my friend anymore. I don't care what Mr. MacClaus said. You cheated."

"I said I was sorry," said Rosie.

"It's too late," said Sally.

So Rosie walked home alone. When she got there, she saw her grandma working in the garden. For a moment, Rosie thought of telling her what had happened. But it was too embarrassing, and Rosie was sure her grandma would scold her for cheating.

So Rosie just said hi, as if nothing was wrong. She went inside the house and fixed herself a snack. She poured herself a glass of milk and put some graham crackers on a plate with ducks around the rim. Sally had given her the plate for her birthday. Rosie looked at the ring of ducks and burst into tears. She ran to her bedroom, flung herself onto her bed, and sobbed.

6.

Sisterly Love

"Is something wrong?" asked a voice. Rosie stopped crying for a moment and looked up from her pillow. It was Jane, peeking through the door to Rosie's bedroom.

"Go away," said Rosie. She started to cry again.

"Are you sick? Are you hurt?" asked Jane.

Rosie turned away from her sister and shook her head. "No. Go away."

Rosie heard Jane come into the room and close the door behind her. She felt the mattress sag as her sister sat on the edge of the bed.

"Go away!" cried Rosie.

Rosie felt a hand on her shoulder. Then Jane dangled a tissue in front of Rosie's face. Rosie grabbed it and wiped her eyes.

"So what's up?" asked Jane.

"Nothing," said Rosie.

"Just tell me a little bit," said Jane. "Otherwise, I'll bring in my tape player and play *The Magic Flute*." *The Magic Flute* was an opera that Jane loved as much as chocolate and Rosie hated as much as pea soup.

Jane dangled another tissue in front of Rosie's face. Rosie took it and blew her nose. Then she turned over and looked at her sister. Jane was wearing one of her worst creations: pegged pants with men's boxer shorts over them and a huge shirt belted with a man's necktie.

Rosie knew when she was trapped. Jane wouldn't leave until Rosie told her the truth.

"Tomorrow is Field Day," she said. "Our team has a dumb name and dumb costumes, and Sally is mad at me." Rosie told Jane about cheating in the race.

Jane didn't laugh. She didn't lecture either. She just looked at Rosie in a sad, nice way and said, "That must have been awful for you."

Rosie felt tears come to her eyes again. It *had* been awful. Jane passed her another tissue, and Rosie blew her nose again. "There's something else," said Rosie.

"What?" asked Jane.

Rosie was afraid to tell Jane what she was thinking. "You might not like it," she said.

"Try me," said Jane.

"Sally's family helps her practice for Field Day. That's why she's so good. No one in our family helps me. Mom's too busy. Grandma doesn't know anything about sports, and you hate them." Rosie burst into tears again.

This time Jane handed her the whole tissue box and said, "I can't speak for Mom and Grandma, but you're right about me. I do hate sports, and I always hated Field Day. I hated the races, I hated the heat, I hated the bugs, I hated the hotdogs, and I always came in last. I never, ever won a single ribbon. Losing bothered me then, but it doesn't anymore. You get over these things. But I tell you what. Since you care so much about Field Day, I'll help you and your teammates with your costumes."

"You will?" Rosie sat up.

"Yes. What's your team's name?"

Rosie was embarrassed to say it. If Jane laughed, Rosie would know the name was dumb, stupid, and uncool.

"Come on," said Jane, smiling. "What is it?"

Rosie took a piece of paper and wrote the name on it.

"The Fabulous Flying Fire Fish?" said Jane. "That's a terrific name! We'll make red satin fins with sequins for everyone, and you can paint gills on your cheeks with lipstick!"

"Can Marco and Chris come over and help make the fins?" asked Rosie.

"Of course," said Jane. "The more the merrier. Maybe Grandma will help too."

Rosie felt wonderful. She couldn't believe her horrible sister Jane was being so nice to her.

Jane's room had two beds in it. One was for sleeping, and the other was piled with cloth, thread, sewing supplies, and patterns. On her desk was a sewing machine. At night Jane had to do her homework sitting on her sleeping bed. Now her sleeping bed became a workplace for Rosie, Marco, and Chris.

Jane gave them red, shiny cloth, scissors, sequins, a needle, thread, glue, and glitter. She cut out cardboard fins at her desk and sewed red fabric to them. Then she passed the fins to the bed, where Rosie, Marco, and Chris finished them by adding glue and glitter.

After a while, Grandma came in and helped too. She sewed ribbons to the fins so the Flying Fish could tie them on their arms.

Rosie was amazed at how quickly Jane could sew on her machine. And her grandma sewed almost as fast by hand.

"How do you do that?" Rosie asked them.

"It takes practice," said Jane. "You can't freak out if you make a mistake."

"You have to be calm and pay attention," said her grandma.

Just like racing, thought Rosie.

7.

Field Day

It was Friday, the big day. In the early morning the skies had been gray, but by eleven the sun had come out. Now it was shining on the third graders and their parents.

Sally still wasn't speaking to Rosie, but Sally's mom and dad and Ben waved hello. Ben flashed Rosie a *V* for victory sign, and Rosie flashed it back to him. She hoped the sign would bring her good luck.

Rosie needed all the luck she could get. She hated to have her best friend mad at her, and she felt bad that no one from her family was there to cheer for her team. Jane had said she might be able to come after high school was out. Her mother had said she might be able to come during her lunch hour. Her grandma had said she might come if she got her petunias planted. But that didn't add up to much.

The third graders stood in two separate lines. All the Ones wore red jerseys. All the Twos wore yellow jerseys. Rosie knew that her team wore red because they were the Fabulous Flying Fire Fish, but she didn't know what the yellow color stood for.

"May the best team win," said Mr. Mac. "And may both teams display good sportsmanship and have a good time. The winners of the name and costume contests will be announced after lunch. All I need to know now are the team names. Team One, what is your name?"

"The Fabulous Flying Fire Fish!" said Chris. Everyone cheered. It *was* a very good name, thought Rosie.

"Team Two," said Mr. Mac. "What is your name?"

"The Killer Bees!" said Sally. Everyone cheered again, and some of the Killer Bees buzzed. Killer Bees was a good name, too, thought Rosie.

"The sack race is the first event," said Mr. Mac. The Fabulous Flying Fire Fish and the

Killer Bees went to the starting line and pulled up their sacks.

"Ready . . . on your mark . . . get set . . . go!" yelled Mr. Mac. Rosie hated the scratchy feel of the sack, but she tried to ignore it. She hopped faster than she ever had in practice. Soon she was ahead of everyone and halfway to the finish line! But then Billy, a Killer Bee, came up next to her. As Rosie tried to go faster, her feet got caught in the sack. She fell down. Billy won. Sally came in second.

One point went to the Killer Bees. The score was 1–0.

The next event was the three-legged race. Rosie's partner was Marco again. They sat together on the starting line waiting for Mr. Mac to tie their ankles together.

"Remember, don't go too fast," said Rosie.

"I know," said Marco. "And start with your inside foot."

"I know," said Rosie.

Mr. Mac tied everyone's ankles together. When he was finished, he stood on the sideline and yelled, "Ready . . . on your mark . . . get set . . . go!"

Rosie started off with her inside foot, but

Marco started with his outside foot. They tripped and fell down on the starting line.

"You used the wrong foot!" yelled Marco.

"I did not! You did!" cried Rosie.

They tried to get up, but they were both so upset that they fell down again. By the time they got going it was too late. The race was over. Sally and Sam had won.

Another point went to the Killer Bees. The score was 2–0.

The next event was the mystery toss. Mr. Mac held up something round and wet wrapped in a towel. "Guess what you're going to be tossing in the mystery toss," he said.

"Beach balls," said Billy.

"Marshmallows," said Chris.

"Balloons," said Rosie.

"Close," said Mr. Mac. Out of the bag he lifted a big, floppy balloon.

"Water balloons!" yelled Sally.

"Correct," said Mr. Mac.

"Yippee!" said Chris. "I hope it breaks and I get all wet. I need to cool off!"

"Some of you will definitely get wet," said Mr. Mac. "I promise. Now, stand facing your partner on the starting line."

The partners lined up. Rosie's partner, unfortunately, was Chris. "Chris," she pleaded. "I know you want to cool off, but please, throw the balloon gently. Let's try to win, okay?"

"Sure," said Chris.

Mr. Mac gave Rosie their water balloon. It was cold and wet and slippery. She had to hold it with both hands.

Mr. Mac blew his whistle. "Ready?" he said. "On your mark . . . get set . . . throw!" Rosie threw the heavy balloon to Chris very carefully. He caught it without breaking it and took one step backward.

"Good!" yelled Rosie.

Chris threw the water balloon back to Rosie. She caught it in her arms as gently as she could. It didn't break. So far so good. Rosie stepped backward, took a deep breath, and heaved the balloon. Chris caught it! He stepped backward and threw it back to Rosie. She caught it. They kept on this way. Each time they caught the balloon, one of them stepped backward.

Lots of other balloons down the line broke, and kids were shrieking as they got all wet. But Rosie and Chris were still dry. Rosie looked around. Sally and Freddy were still dry too. Soon Rosie and Chris and Sally and Freddy were the only four people left in the event. "We might win this!" Rosie yelled to Chris. "Pay attention!" She threw Chris the water balloon really carefully. He caught it and stepped backward. Now it was his turn to throw it to her.

"Here it comes!" yelled Chris. He threw the balloon way up in the air. It went higher than it had ever gone before. Rosie had her eyes right on it, and she knew she could catch it, but wasn't it coming down too fast? Could she catch it without breaking it?

Splat! The balloon hit her arms and burst open. Water splashed everywhere, and Rosie got soaked. Chris hooted with laughter.

Freddy threw his balloon to Sally, who caught it without breaking it. That was it. They had won the balloon toss. Rosie wished she had three giant water balloons to dump on Sally, Freddy, and her wonderful teammate Chris, who was still laughing.

One more point went to the Killer Bees. The score was now 3–zip.

8.

Sally Smiles Again

Rosie sat in a patch of sunlight near the trees where the parents were serving lunch. She was wet and unhappy. The other kids were lining up for food, but Rosie didn't join them. The thought of hotdogs, pizza, popcorn, watermelon, and fruit punch made her feel sick. Nevertheless, after a while she went over and took a slice of pizza and a cup of punch. Then she went back to sit alone in her little patch of sun.

"Can I sit down too?" someone asked.

Rosie looked up. It was Sally. "I guess so," said Rosie.

Sally sat down with a grin. "I decided I'm not mad at you anymore," she said. "Isn't this fun?"

Rosie pretended she couldn't talk because her mouth was full.

"I said, isn't this fun?"

Rosie swallowed. Then she looked straight at Sally and said, "It's fun for you because you always win."

Sally's smile faded. She got up and said, "Forget I ever came over to talk to you, creep."

Rosie felt worse than ever now, but she had to get up and join her team. It was time to put

on the costumes. The costumes were in grocery bags at the side of the field. As Rosie unpacked them, everyone said the fins looked neat. Then her team helped each other put them on. Rosie thought the fins looked good too, but she still felt terrible.

Across the grass the Killer Bees were putting on their costumes—big, floppy yellow paper wings and long yellow feelers. Rosie watched to see if Sally was looking at her, but Sally didn't glance over once.

When the teams were ready, Mr. Mac blew his whistle, and the parade began. Each team had to march single file past a panel of teachers.

The Killer Bees went first. They had wrapped black tape around their jerseys for bee stripes and painted black stripes on their faces. As they walked by the judges, they flapped their arms and buzzed.

"Their wings droop," said Chris. "They should have made them out of cloth and cardboard like us. But listen to them. Don't they sound great?"

"Too bad fish don't make noise," said Marco.

"But they do!" said Chris. "Listen." He started a chant, moving his fins in time to it. "Swish, swish, bubble, bubble. Swish, swish, bubble, bubble." Everyone else on the team copied him.

"Swish, swish, bubble, bubble" went the Fabulous Flying Fire Fish as they passed before the judges. Rosie made the fish noise, too, but her heart wasn't in it. She kept thinking about her fight with Sally.

When the parade was over, the leader of the teachers' panel stood up. "Both teams have great costumes this year," she said, "so it was very hard to reach a decision. However, we have decided that first prize for costumes goes to . . . the Fabulous Flying Fire Fish!" The Fire Fish jumped up and down with happiness. All except Rosie. She just jumped up and down.

The score was now 3 to 1.

Mr. Mac held up a box. "All the teachers voted this morning on the team names," he said. "They put their votes in this box. I have counted them and would like to announce that first prize goes to . . . the Fabulous Flying Fire Fish!" The Fire Fish jumped up and down with happiness again. All except Rosie.

The score was now 3–2.

"Next we come to the award for good sportsmanship," said Mr. Mac. "All morning the Killer Bees won. That was great for them but very hard on the other team. But the Flying Fish didn't quit or cheat. So the Sportsmanship Award goes to . . . the Fabulous Flying Fire Fish!"

For the third time in a row the Fire Fish jumped up and down. And this time, even though Rosie was still worried about Sally, she felt a small thrill of excitement. The score was now tied 3–3, and it was time for the big race.

9.

The Big Race

Rosie knew she had to do something to save her friendship with Sally. So she went up to the starting line and stood next to her friend. "Hi," she said.

"Hi," said Sally. "Happy now because your team won some points?"

Rosie nodded. "Yes."

"Winning is fun, isn't it?" said Sally. "What did you do—bribe the teachers?"

"Oh, Sally, please," said Rosie. "Don't be mad at me anymore. You're my best friend, and I want to wish you good luck in the race. You'll probably beat me, and that's okay. I just want you to know that whatever happens, you're still my best friend."

"Really and truly?" asked Sally.

"Really and truly," said Rosie.

"Then you're my best friend too," said Sally
with a smile. "It's no fun being mad at you. I
hope you run a good race too. Good luck."

Rosie smiled. All her jitters disappeared.
Now she felt peaceful and calm.

Mr. Mac blew his whistle. "Ready!" he
shouted.

The ten runners got in position.

"On your mark."

They got down.

"Get set."

They got up on their toes.

"Go!"

Off went the ten runners. They all got a good
start because they were all good racers. Sally
and Rosie were together at first, but then Sally
pulled ahead. Rosie watched her best friend
with mixed feelings. She was happy that she
and Sally were friends again, but the truth was
that she was also a little disappointed to see
her friend winning.

"The most important thing is to enjoy a race,"
Ben had said. And it was true, Rosie did love
to run. She loved it even now, with all her mixed
feelings.

Ben had also said to concentrate and save

your energy as if it were money. Rosie was running fast, but she wasn't running her very fastest. Sam and Sally were in front of her. Maybe one of them was spending too much energy.

Rosie put on just a little more speed. As she did, she came up next to Sam. They rounded the corner of the track where Rosie had cheated. This time Rosie stayed on the course.

Up ahead was Sally.

I might be able to catch up with her, thought Rosie, starting to go a little bit faster. Far ahead she could see the finish line, where people were cheering.

Rosie heard a voice rise out from the crowd. "Come on, Rosie!" It was Jane yelling. "You're doing fine! Pour it on!"

Rosie started to run faster. She passed Sam on the homestretch. Sally was just a little bit ahead of her. Rosie heard another voice. "Go, Rosie, go!" It was Grandma!

In a great burst of speed Rosie caught up with Sally. She could hear Sam behind her, but she didn't turn to look at him. Instead, she concentrated on winning. She still had a little extra energy left because she hadn't spent it all earlier.

She and Sally were neck and neck.

"Go, Poodle! Go, Toodle!" cried another familiar voice. It was Ben, cheering for both girls.

"Give it all you've got!" yelled someone else. It was Rosie's mother!

Rosie pumped her legs harder and harder and harder. At the last moment she burst past Sally and won the race.

"HOORAY ROSIE!" yelled the Fabulous Flying Fire Fish. Jane ran up and slapped her high fives. Mr. Mac shouted, "Congratulations, Rosie!" Her mother and grandma were beaming with pride.

Rosie felt herself being lifted high into the air. Ben had swung her up to the sky in his strong arms. She felt absolutely terrific.

Then, just as Ben swung her down to the ground, Rosie thought of Sally. Where was she? Did she feel terrible? She had never lost a race before. Rosie looked around at all the smiling faces as her mother and grandma both gave her a kiss at the same time.

"Thanks," she said. "But excuse me for a minute."

Rosie found Sally off to the side of the crowd, having a drink of punch with her parents. Her mom had her arm around her, and her father was taking her photograph, but Sally didn't look very happy.

"Hey, Rosie!" cried Sally's mom. "Come on over and get in the picture!"

"Are you sure you want me?" asked Rosie.

"Of course I'm sure," said Sally's mom.

"Is Sally sure?" asked Rosie.

Sally's face broke into a little grin. "Sure, I'm sure," she said. "Congratulations."

Sally and Rosie put their arms around each other and said "Cheese" for the camera.

• • •

The award ceremony was about to begin. Rosie and Sally went over to where everyone was waiting under the trees.

Rosie sat down on the grass next to Sally. She felt wonderful. She had won a race, the Fabulous Flying Fire Fish had won Field Day, and best of all, she and Sally were friends again.

That night Rosie pinned her first-place ribbon up on her bulletin board. It was the prettiest color blue she had ever seen.

It was true blue.

About the Author

"When my sons were younger," says author Jean Marzollo, "they were always looking for sports stories. That's one of the reasons I started writing them. I loved sports too when I was a kid. I still do, actually. I'm always listening to New York's all-sports radio station, and in my next life I hope to be either a violin player or a major league shortstop."

Jean Marzollo has written dozens of books for young readers. She lives with her husband and two sons in Cold Spring, New York.

About the Illustrator

"I was a real tomboy when I was little," says illustrator Blanche Sims. "I loved all sports, especially running. I was a star runner and often came in first. But lots of times I came in second, too, just like Rosie."

Blanche Sims has illustrated many books for children, including *Soccer Sam* and *Cannonball Chris,* both by Jean Marzollo. She lives in Westport, Connecticut.